MW00973269

WORKBOOK

John Wiltshier • José Luis Morales
Series Advisor: David Nunan

Series Consultants:
Hilda Martínez • Xóchitl Arvizu

Advisory Board:
Tim Budden • Tina Chen • Betty Deng
Aaron Jolly • Dr. Nam-Joon Kang
Dr. Wonkey Lee • Wenxin Liang
Ann Mayeda • Wade O. Nichols
Jamie Zhang

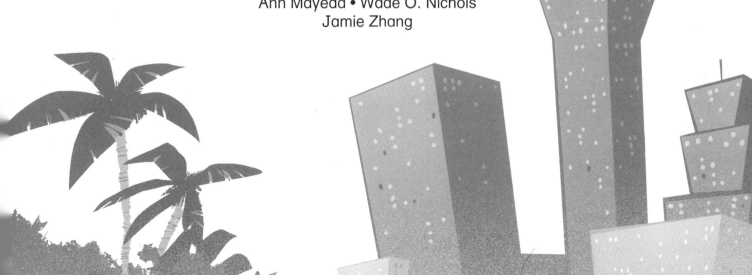

Pearson Education Limited
Edinburgh Gate
Harlow
Essex CM20 2JE
England
and Associated Companies throughout the world.

Our Discovery Island ™

www.ourdiscoveryisland.com

© Pearson Education Limited 2012

The rights of John Wiltshier, José Luis Morales, and Linnette Ansel Erocak to be identified as authors of this work have been asserted by them in accordance with the Copyright, Designs and Patents Act 1988.

First published 2012
Third impression 2012

ISBN: 978-1-4479-0072-6

Set in Longman English 12.5/20pt
Printed in China (CTPS/03)

Illustrators: Leo Cultura, Mark Draisey, Michael Garton (The Bright Agency), John Haslam, Ned Jolliffe, Simone Massoni (Advocate), Moira Millman, Ken Mok, Rui Ricardo (Folio), and Olimpia Wong

Picture Credits: The publisher would like to thank the following for their kind permission to reproduce their photographs: (Key: b-bottom; c-centre; l-left; r-right; t-top) Alamy Images: Oliver Gerhard 22, Jeff Morgan 01 33tr, Radius Images 42bl; Art Directors and TRIP Photo Library: John Wallace 33c; Corbis: Jim Craigmyle 52, Image Source 42r, Juice Images 32l, Science Faction / Steven Kazlowski 23t; Getty Images: Taxi / Eri Morita 42tl; iStockphoto: Jani Bryson 62; Pearson Education Ltd: Jules Selmes 11, Studio 8 16cl; Shutterstock.com: Atlaspix 71tl, Paul Banton 21cl, Paul Coartney 21cr, Comosaydice 21l, David Davis 16r, East 32r, Four Oaks 26cr, Karel Gallas 26r, Cathy Keifer 23b, Jan Kratochvila 26l, Ivan Kuzmin 21c, Marie Lumiere 26cl, R. Gino Santa Maria 16cr, Joe Mercier 71br, Nulinukas 71tr, Photobar 21r, Lesley Rigg 71bl, Schalke Fotografie / Melissa Schalke 16l, Szefei 61; Thinkstock: iStockphoto 33tl, and Stockbyte 82.

All other images © Pearson Education

Every effort has been made to trace the copyright holders and we apologise in advance for any unintentional omissions. We would be pleased to insert the appropriate acknowledgement in any subsequent edition of this publication.

Contents

Welcome

1 **Write the names of the characters.**

> Marta   Chris   Champ   Serena   Zero Zendell

1

2

3

_____

4

5

_____

2 **Look at Activity 1 and number.**

a He's Marta's friend. He's very smart and he likes to study. He hates getting dirty so he usually plays indoors. ☐

b She's brave and lives in a nature reserve with her parents. Her parents work there so sometimes she helps. She has a great friend. His name is Champ. ☐

c He was in a tree and wild dogs were trying to attack him. Marta's dad rescued him from the tree. Marta gave him his name and she looks after him. He's happy and always friendly. ☐

d He always wears a top hat and he has a long mustache. He's the only person who has animals on Future Island, but this year not many people are coming to his zoo. ☐

e She's a girl from the future. She's good at running and jumping, and she can climb walls! She's usually outside. ☐

3  Check (✔).

1 Who has a zoo?

2 Who lives on Future Island?

4 Circle T = True or F = False.

1 Marta's dad rescues Champ from a tree. T / F

2 Marta lives with her mom and dad in the nature reserve. T / F

3 The name of the nature reserve is "Elephant Rock". T / F

4 Marta is the chimpanzee's new dad. T / F

5 The number of visitors to the zoo is going up. T / F

6 Zero Zendell doesn't know what to do. T / F

5 What do you think Zero Zendell is planning? Write 1 to 4.
(1 = very probable, 4 = not probable)

a He's planning to show films of animals from the past.

b He's planning to travel to the past to steal animals and bring them to the future.

c He's planning to close the zoo and open a water park.

d He's planning to show robot animals.

6  **Match.**

1   1st   a   forty-second

2   7th   b   thirteenth

3   13th   c   ninety-ninth

4   20th   d   seventh

5   28th   e   sixty-fifth

6   42nd   f   twentieth

7   65th   g   first

8   99th   h   twenty-eighth

7 (02) **Listen and circle.**

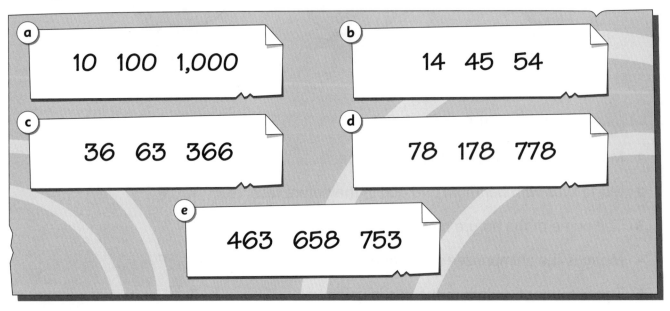

a   10   100   1,000

b   14   45   54

c   36   63   366

d   78   178   778

e   463   658   753

8  **Write.**

1   first, second, third, _farth, fiths sixth_

2   fifteenth, sixteenth, _seventeenth_, eighteenth

3   twentieth, _____, fortieth, fiftieth

4   eleventh, twenty-first, thirty-first, _____

5   sixty-sixth, sixty-seventh, _____, sixty-ninth

6   _____, ninety-eighth, ninety-seventh, ninety-sixth

9 Write.

| furry   sweet   loud   hard   cold   spiky |

1 The ice is _____ .

2 The chocolate is _____ .

3 The music is _____ .

4 The hair is _____ .

5 The spider is _____ .

6 The rock is _____ .

10 Think and write.

1 Shells are _____ smooth.

2 _____ round.

3 _____ soft.

4 _____ scary.

5 _____ cute.

6 _____ loud.

11 Listen and check (✓). Then write.

| chocolate   a fish   a rose   a soft toy lion |

	looks	feels	smells	sounds	tastes	What is it?
1	wet ☐ scary ☐	rough ☐ cold ☐	like the sea ☐ like a lemon ☐			_____
2		soft ☐ hard ☐		scary ☐ nice ☐		_____
3	brown ☐ black ☐	smooth ☐ sharp ☐	great ☐ bad ☐		sour ☐ sweet ☐	_____
4	beautiful ☐ bad ☐	furry ☐ spiky ☐	sweet ☐ good ☐			

1 Adventure camp

1 Write the names of the characters.

Hannah   Tom   Felipe   Flo   Maria

1 _____

2 _____

3 _____

4 _____

5 _____

2 Unscramble the letters and write. Then number.

1 ttne   _____

2 slepo   _____

3 geps   _____

4 thaflishgl   _____

5 pomcssa   _____

6 isleengp gba _____

a ▢

b ▢

c ▢

d ▢

e ▢

f ▢

3 04 Look at Flo's list. Listen and write ✓ or ✗.

List for Adventure camp

a backpack ▢   books ▢

a flashlight ▢   an mp3 player ▢

pegs ▢   a sleeping bag ▢

a compass ▢

4 ✏️ **Circle.**

1 I like (play / playing) soccer, but I (don't / doesn't) like camping.

2 He doesn't like (watch / watching) TV. He (like / likes) reading.

3 They're (Brazil / British). They're (live / from) the United Kingdom.

4 We're good (at dancing / dancing). We (never / always) practice.

5 She loves trampolining and (ski / skiing). She thinks they're (fun / boring).

6 He's good (at singing / at sing). He's a famous (soldier / musician).

5 💿05 **Listen and circle.**

1 Tom has one (sister / brother).

2 Maria likes dancing, but she's not good at (singing / swimming).

3 Flo is from the (United States / United Kingdom). She's good at (skiing / swimming) and she loves talking to friends.

4 Felipe likes science and (English / math).

6 ✏️ **Draw yourself. Then write.**

My name's _____.

I'm from _____

in _____.

I love _____

and _____,

but I don't like _____

_____.

I'm good at _____

and _____,

but I'm not good at _____.

7  **Number.**

a

1 They're lighting a fire.

2 He's laying out the bed.

3 They're covering their heads.

4 He's putting in the pegs.

5 She's reading a compass.

6 They're taking down the tent.

7 It's keeping out the rain.

8 They're pitching the tent.

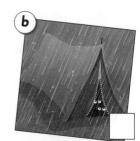
b

c

d

e

f

g

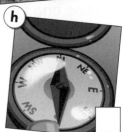
h

8  **Write.**

1 The dog is running _____.

2 The two boys _____.

3 The girl _____.

4 The man _____.

5 The two girls _____.

06 **Sing.** (See Student Book page 14.)

9 🎧 **07 Listen and circle.**

1 I (can / can't) read a book, but I (can / can't) read a map.

2 They (can / can't) swim, but they (can / can't) pitch a tent.

3 They (can / can't) put in the pegs, (and / but) they can light a fire.

4 She likes reading comic books, (and / but) she (can / can't) read a compass.

5 We can pitch a tent, (and / but) we (can / can't) take down a tent, too.

10 🎧 **08 Listen and write what Sandy can and can't do.**

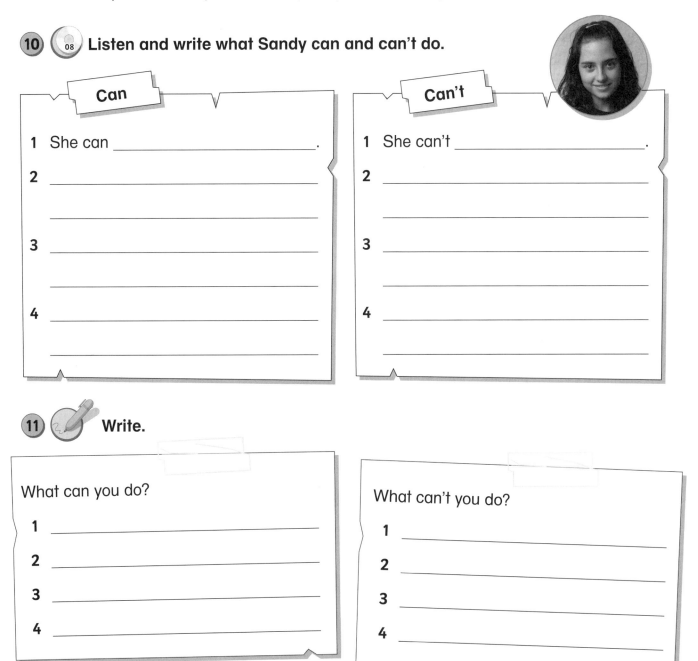

Can	Can't
1 She can _____.	**1** She can't _____.
2 _____	**2** _____
3 _____	**3** _____
4 _____	**4** _____

11 ✏️ **Write.**

What can you do?

1 _____

2 _____

3 _____

4 _____

What can't you do?

1 _____

2 _____

3 _____

4 _____

12  **Listen and write.**

Hello Grandpa,

How are you and ¹_____? Adventure camp is great. It's my

third day here. I have some new friends from ²_____

and Mexico. They're really nice. I'm teaching ³_____ to my

new friend, Flo. She's funny. I like her but she's not good at learning Spanish!

Our first day was good. There was a big dinner and then there were songs by

the campfire. I don't like ⁴_____, but it was fun. Bed was late.

Tonight I want to go to bed early!

Yesterday, we ⁵_____ for a walk in the forest. It's very

beautiful here. There ⁶_____ any computers and there

⁷_____ any Internet, but I ⁸_____ the camp.

Felipe

13 **Look at Activity 12 and write.**

1 Who is the letter for?

_____

2 Is it Felipe's second day?

_____

3 What did Felipe do yesterday?

_____

 **14** Write.

15 Write. Use the words from Activity 14.

1 Bear Grylls usually lives in the United Kingdom, but sometimes he lives in the desert, the _____, or the jungle.

2 Bear Grylls likes playing the _____.

3 There are often a lot of _____ and insects in the jungle.

4 Bear Grylls sometimes sleeps up a _____ in the jungle.

5 His favorite place is an _____ in Indonesia.

6 Bear Grylls runs a lot and does _____.

7 The _____ is a difficult place to live in.

8 Bear Grylls is a _____ and an adventurer.

16  **Check (✓).**

1 Where are Marta and Chris after traveling in the time machine?

☐ the nature reserve

☐ a city in the future

☐ Zero Zendell's zoo

2 Who has Champ?

☐ Marta and Chris

☐ Marta's dad

☐ Zero Zendell

17 **Circle.**

1 Marta and Chris are going ….

a to the park **b** to the amusement park **c** to school

2 Marta and Chris think the time machine is ….

a scary **b** boring **c** cool

3 To go into the time machine costs ….

a three dollars **b** ten dollars **c** a dollar

4 Chris doesn't like ….

a Zero Zendell **b** Marta **c** Champ

18 **Find and read Zero Zendell's code.**

EHMYESGERCSSIT

TƵIƵ IƵ MƵ SƵCƵEƵ MƵSƵAƵE ƵAƵHƵNƵ.

19 **Find and write the question. Then write the answer.**

RAHCIP

WƵEƵE ƵS ƵHƵMƵ?

_____

_____

_____

_____

14

 **20** **Match.**

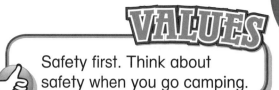
VALUES **1**

Safety first. Think about safety when you go camping.

Situation

1 When you get into a car …

2 In rocky places on the coast …

3 At home …

4 In a swimming pool …

5 In windy, stormy weather …

6 During take off and landing on a plane …

The safe thing to do

a Fasten your seatbelt!

b Look before you dive!

f Don't stand under trees!

e Don't use electrical things near water!

d Don't dive or swim!

c Buckle up!

 **21** **Write ✗ for the activities you don't want to try.**

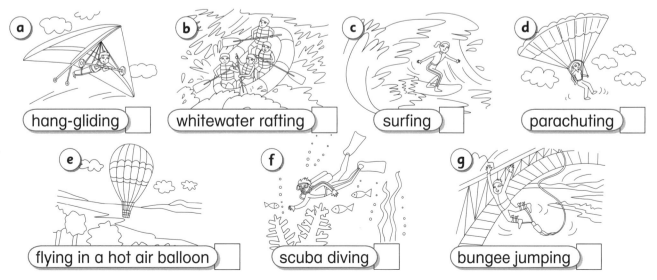

a hang-gliding

b whitewater rafting

c surfing

d parachuting

e flying in a hot air balloon

f scuba diving

g bungee jumping

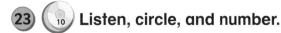

22 **Match.**

1 poles		**a**	this tells you where north is
2 tent		**b**	put a bed on the floor
3 sleeping bag		**c**	use this to see in the dark
4 pegs		**d**	this keeps you warm at night
5 flashlight		**e**	do this to start a fire
6 lay out		**f**	a house you can take with you
7 cover		**g**	you can carry clothes and books in this
8 light		**h**	use these to stop a tent flying away
9 compass		**i**	use these to support a tent
10 backpack		**j**	put something over something

23 **Listen, circle, and number.**

Ron

Jo

Brad

Jackie

a I can pitch a tent, (but / and) I (can / can't) read a compass. ☐

b I like lighting fires, (but / and) I (like / don't like) cooking. ☐

c I love hiking with a flashlight at night, (but / and) I (love / don't love) camping under the stars. ☐

d I (like / don't like) walking in the rain, (but / and) I usually cover my head. ☐

24 **Unscramble and write. Then write Yes or No for you.**

1 mom / tennis / at / good / my / playing / is

_____ Is it true? _____

2 like swimming / I / I / don't like running / but

_____ Is it true? _____

3 loves / my / fishing / father

_____ Is it true? _____

16

25 **11** **Listen and write.**

Two people I love are my mother and my brother. My [1]_____ is good at

baseball. He plays every day. My [2]_____ isn't good at baseball. She can't

throw and [3]_____ hit. She [4]_____ sporty. She loves

[5]_____ romantic books and likes [6]_____ dramas on TV. My

brother [7]_____ like romantic movies or books, [8]_____ he

loves action movies. He isn't [9]_____ math and my mom can't

[10]_____ because she isn't good at math, either!

26 **Write about two people.**

What are they good at? What do they like doing? What do they love doing?
What are they not good at? What don't they like doing?

Two people I love are _____ and _____ .

_____

_____

_____

_____

_____

_____

_____

_____

_____

2 Wildlife park

1 Unscramble and write. Then match.

a

1 trote _____
2 egrit _____
3 sale _____
4 eas tutelr _____

b

5 eawlh _____
6 hcthaee _____

c

7 melur _____
8 retpahn _____

d

9 alkoa _____
10 orinh _____

e

f

g

h

i

j

2 Write about the animals in Activity 1.

| heavy | scary | big | fast | slow |

1 Cheetahs are fast. _____
2 _____
3 _____
4 _____
5 _____

3 🔘12 Listen and write. Then match.

1 210 _____
2 _____
3 _____
4 _____
5 _____
6 _____
7 _____
8 _____

a two thousand ten
b three hundred seventy
c six hundred forty-two
d two hundred ten
e two hundred eighteen
f one hundred eighty
g one thousand eighteen
h four thousand seventeen

4 (13) **Listen and write.**

		How tall?	How heavy?	How long?
1		1.2 meters	_____ kilograms	2.5 meters
2		_____ meters	60 kilograms	_____ meters
3			_____ kilograms	_____ meters
4		_____ meters	_____ kilograms	_____ meters
5		_____ meters	_____ kilograms	_____ meters

5 **Unscramble and write questions.**

1 hippo / is / long / how / the _____

2 tall / how / lion / is / the _____

3 the / heavy / snake / how / is _____

4 long / how / is / the / elephant _____

5 cheetah / how / tall / is / the _____

6 **Look at Activity 4 and write answers to the questions in Activity 5.**

1 The hippo is 4 meters long. _____

2 _____

3 _____

4 _____

5 _____

7 **Write.**

1 big   _____bigger_____   _____biggest_____   2 tall   _____ _____

3 heavy _____ _____   4 slow   _____ _____

5 short _____ _____   6 small   _____ _____

7 fast   _____ _____   8 light   _____ _____

9 long   _____ _____

8 **Write.**

1 The lemur _is faster than the tiger_____. (fast)

2 The panther _____.(big)

3 The whale _____.(long)

4 The whale _____.(heavy)

5 The seal _____.(small)

6 The turtle _____.(slow)

9 **Write questions. Then look at Activity 8 and write the answers.**

1 panther / fast / lemur

Is the panther faster than the lemur?   _No, it isn't._

2 turtle / fast / otter

_____   _____

3 whale / heavy / sea turtle

_____   _____

20

10 **Write.**

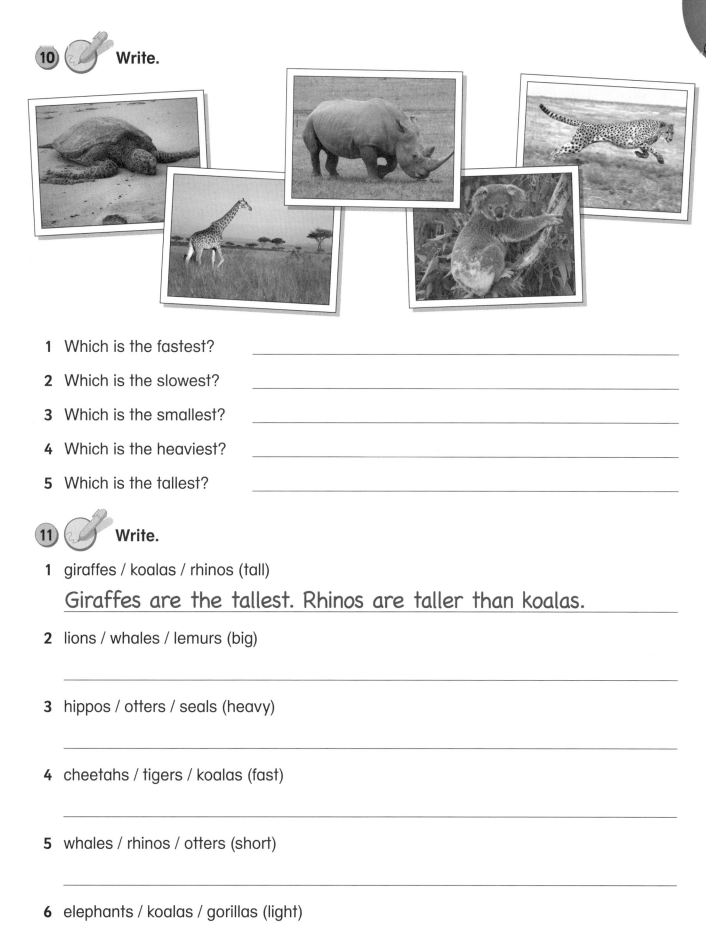

1 Which is the fastest? _____

2 Which is the slowest? _____

3 Which is the smallest? _____

4 Which is the heaviest? _____

5 Which is the tallest? _____

11 **Write.**

1 giraffes / koalas / rhinos (tall)

Giraffes are the tallest. Rhinos are taller than koalas.

2 lions / whales / lemurs (big)

_____

3 hippos / otters / seals (heavy)

_____

4 cheetahs / tigers / koalas (fast)

_____

5 whales / rhinos / otters (short)

_____

6 elephants / koalas / gorillas (light)

_____

12  **Listen and circle.**

1 Mike (likes / doesn't like) the Koala reserve.

2 Vernie is (7 meters / 70 centimeters) tall.

3 Vernie likes (running / sleeping).

4 Vernie is (8 / 80) kilograms.

5 Mike wants to sponsor (Jen / Vernie).

13 **Listen again and order the questions. Then write the answers.**

a How tall is Vernie? ☐ _____

b Can I ask you some questions? ☐ _____

c Can she run? ☐ _____

d How heavy is she? ☐ _____

e How fast is she? ☐ _____

f Do you like the koala reserve? ☐1 Yes, I do. _____

g So, why all the questions? ☐ _____

14 **Write. Then circle T = True, F = False, or S = Sometimes.**

1 Giraffes are _____taller_____ (tall) than lions. T / F / S

2 Rhinos are _____ (heavy) than cheetahs. T / F / S

3 Cheetahs are _____ (short) than elephants. T / F / S

4 Sea turtles are _____ (big) than whales. T / F / S

5 Crocodiles are _____ (long) than snakes. T / F / S

6 Elephants are _____ (slow) than cheetahs. T / F / S

7 Seals are _____ (small) than rabbits. T / F / S

8 Monkeys are _____ (light) than whales. T / F / S

9 Turtles are _____ (fast) than gorillas. T / F / S

15 16 **Listen and write.**

SEARCH

Cool camouflage in the cold!

Size They are not very heavy and they are not very big. Their tails are usually about 30 centimeters long.

Body Arctic foxes have short legs and short ears. Their coats and tails are very thick and warm—good for living in the snow!

Color Their coats are very good camouflage. They are white when it is snowy in the winter. In the summer, their coats are darker and change to brown or gray. It is difficult to see the foxes next to the brown rocks.

Places Arctic foxes live only in the Arctic, for example in Canada and Greenland. It is very cold there. They can live in temperatures of -50 degrees Celsius.

Food Arctic foxes eat birds, fish, and sometimes vegetables. They are good at catching birds—they are very fast! They often put food in the snow and then eat it later in the year.

1 Arctic foxes have white coats in _____.

2 Arctic foxes have brown coats in _____.

16 **Write c (chameleon) or f (fox).**

1 This animal changes color when it is nervous. ☐

2 This animal lives in very cold places. ☐

3 This animal sometimes eats fish. ☐

4 This animal has a very long tongue. ☐

17 **Think about a wild animal that uses camouflage. Write and draw.**

Animal		Size		
Body		Color		
Places		Food		

18 **Write.**

blue Serena friend light

This is ¹_____. She has ²_____ hair and she's wearing ³_____ clothes. She's Chris and Marta's new ⁴_____.

19  **Find and circle seven mistakes.**

Marta and Chris meet Sarah. She thinks they are poor because they have a cat. Zero Zendell wants animals at any time. The children are in a nature park. The guards look after them. The girl doesn't want to help Marta and Chris.

20 **Check (✓).**

1 Who can't Marta and Chris find?

2 Who wants to help Marta and Chris?

21 (17) **Listen and write.**

NATURE MUSEUM

1 Don't sit _____ on the grass _____.

2 Don't _____ in the museum.

3 Don't _____ the _____.

4 Don't give food or _____ to the animals.

5 Don't take _____ of the animals.

RULES

22  **Write.**

 VALUES

Think before you act. Think carefully before making important decisions.

	1	2	3
Situation A You're planning a birthday party for a friend. What's the easiest way to invite everyone?	Send text messages to all your friends. (You don't have all the cell phone numbers.)	Put up a notice on the school notice board with date, place, and time.	Send everyone a message online. Not everyone is on online. You invite these people tomorrow at school.
_____ is easier than _____. _____ is the _____.			
Situation B You're near a river and a friend falls into the water. He can't swim. You can't swim. What's the smartest thing to do?	Jump into the river.	Call for help and wait for someone to arrive.	Call for help. You find a tree branch and try to help your friend.
_____ is smarter than _____. _____ is the _____.			
Situation C An old friend is in town. You want to do something this weekend. What's the best thing to do?	Invite your friend to dinner at your home. You ask your family first.	Plan a party at your home with two other friends. You don't ask your family first.	Plan a guided tour of your city with friends. You ask your family first.
_____ is better than _____. _____ is the _____.			

23  **Write about a decision you made and how you did it.**

1 I decided to _____ .

_____

2 Was it a good decision?

_____

24 **Match.**

1 heavy
2 short
3 tall
4 fast
5 camouflage
6 sea turtle
7 otter
8 seal
9 tiger
10 koala

a opposite of slow
b an Australian animal that some people think is cute
c opposite of long
d an animal that can't walk but is good at swimming
e a good swimmer that lives in rivers and has a long tail
f a water animal that has a hard shell
g animals use this for safety
h opposite of light
i a cat with striped fur
j opposite of short

25 **Circle.**

1 How (heavy / heavier) is the elephant? It's 2,000 (kilograms / meters).

2 How (long / longer) is it? It's 2.5 meters (long / longer).

3 The panther is (bigger / biggest) than the koala.

4 The sea turtle is the (shorter / shortest).

5 Are giraffes (taller / tallest) than otters?   (Yes, they are. / No, they aren't.)

6 Are rhinos (heavy / heavier) than lemurs?   (Yes, they are. / No, they aren't.)

7 Are panthers (faster / fastest) than cheetahs? (Yes, they are. / No, they aren't.)

8 Are lemurs (small / smaller) than whales?   (Yes, they are. / No, they aren't.)

26 **Number.**

a Which is the heaviest land animal in the world?

b Which is the tallest animal in the world?

c Which is the fastest land animal in the world?

d Which is the longest animal in the world?

27 (18) **Listen and write.**

2

SEARCH

My favorite animal is the hippo. At the ¹_____ I can watch the hippos for

an hour! They are really ²_____ animals. When they walk they are very

³_____. ⁴_____ heavy is a hippo? One hippo weighs

between 1,500 and 3,000 ⁵_____. Hippos are the third ⁶_____

animal in the world (elephants and rhinos are ⁷_____ than hippos).

Hippos can swim. They are ⁸_____ swimmers and they look beautiful in

the water. Hippos enjoy water and having baths. They have small ears, but very big

mouths and big ⁹_____. A hippo's mouth is ¹⁰_____.

28 **Write about your favorite animal.**

3 Where we live

1 Write the places. Then find.

1

_____

2

_____

3

_____

4

_____

5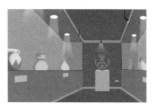

_____

6

_____

s	h	o	p	p	i	n	g	m	a	l	l	k	n	l
r	e	s	r	m	f	a	q	s	t	p	j	c	p	f
l	t	d	c	r	q	l	a	g	y	u	d	b	a	e
i	w	m	o	v	i	e	t	h	e	a	t	e	r	m
b	u	v	s	x	w	i	o	h	z	h	i	c	k	d
r	v	n	i	q	b	y	p	g	k	z	v	a	n	o
a	s	c	r	m	u	s	e	u	m	o	p	l	e	y
r	a	j	t	i	x	k	h	l	m	g	b	w	x	f
y	p	u	s	u	p	e	r	m	a	r	k	e	t	o

2 Write. Use the words from Activity 1.

1 I can buy juice in a _____.

2 I can find interesting books in a _____.

3 I can have a picnic in a _____.

4 I can see old things in a _____.

5 I can watch a movie in a _____.

6 I can buy some clothes in a _____.

3 (19) **Listen and write.**

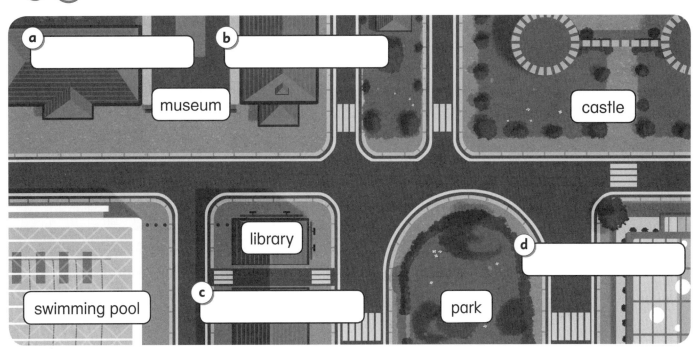

a

b

museum

castle

library

d

swimming pool

c

park

4 **Look at the map in Activity 3 and write.**

1 museum / school   The museum is next to the school.

_____

2 movie theater / library   _____

_____

3 museum / supermarket / school   _____

_____

4 shopping mall / castle   _____

_____

5 supermarket / museum / swimming pool   _____

_____

5 **Write directions from the nearest bus stop to your home.**

Get off the bus and _____.

_____

_____

6 Write.

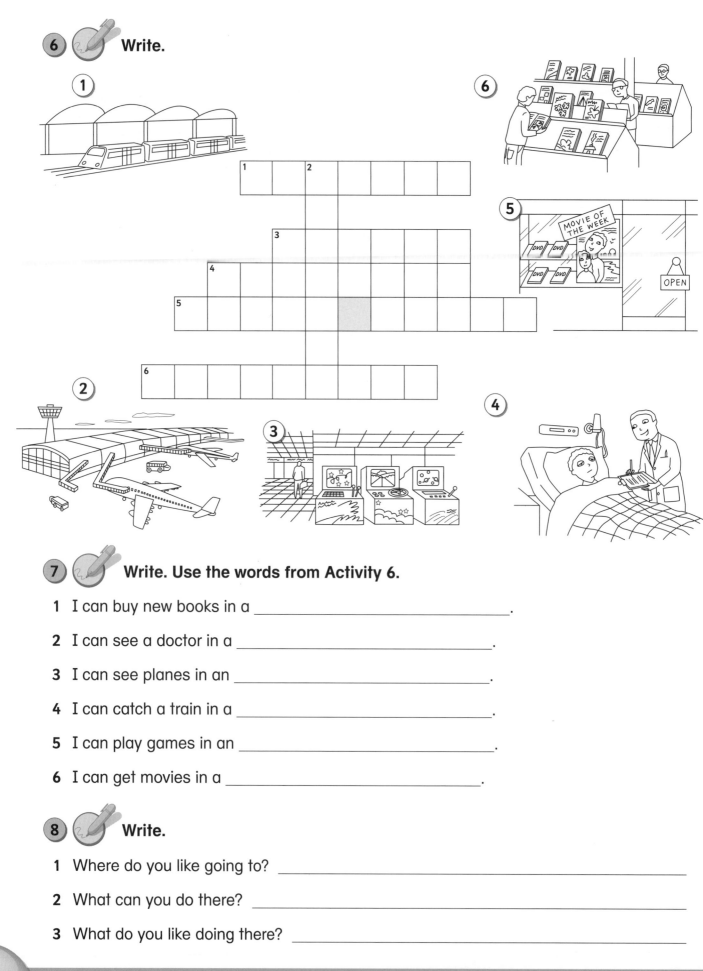

7 Write. Use the words from Activity 6.

1 I can buy new books in a _____.

2 I can see a doctor in a _____.

3 I can see planes in an _____.

4 I can catch a train in a _____.

5 I can play games in an _____.

6 I can get movies in a _____.

8 Write.

1 Where do you like going to? _____

2 What can you do there? _____

3 What do you like doing there? _____

9 ✎ **Write.**

1 Tom / go / park / ✗

Tom doesn't want to go to the park.

2 Flo / meet / in town for lunch / Sunday / ✓

_____

3 Felipe / see / a movie / Saturday / ✗

_____

4 Maria / play basketball / this afternoon / ✗

_____

10 (21) **Look at Activity 9 and write the questions. Then listen and write the answers.**

1
Hi, Tom. Do you want to go to the park?

No, sorry. I have to go shopping to buy a new computer.

2
Hi, Flo. _____

Yes, _____.

3
Hi, Felipe. _____

No, sorry. I have _____.

4
Hi, Maria. _____

No, sorry. _____

11 **22** **Listen and order the sentences 1–5.**

a Do you want to come to Seoul in the summer? ☐

b I don't like quiet places! ☐

c I live near a big park with lots of trees and flowers. ☐

d I want to be good at everything! ☐

e Thanks for your email. It was really interesting! ☐

Alex

Sun-kwan

12 **22** **Circle. Then listen again and check your answers.**

1 Alex (wants / doesn't want) to know more about Seoul.

2 Sun-kwan (likes / doesn't like) quiet places.

3 There's a river (opposite / behind) Sun-kwan's house.

4 Sun-kwan (wants / doesn't want) to go to Sark one day.

13 **Write and, but, or because.**

1 I don't like the city _____ it's too noisy.

2 She wants to go to bed _____ she's tired.

3 He likes going to the library, _____ he doesn't like going to the castle.

4 My village is clean, _____ it isn't beautiful.

5 I like surfing _____ snorkeling.

14 **Write about where you live.**

I like my city because _____ .

In _____ there are _____ and _____ .

There are _____ but there aren't any _____ .

15  **Write.**

bridge   chimney   hill   river   roof

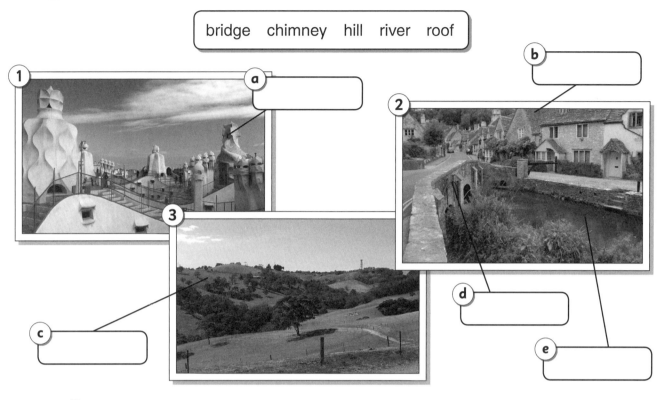

1

a

b

2

3

c

d

e

16 **Number to match the paragraphs a–c to the pictures in Activity 15. Then write.**

Australia   next   because   park   bridge
village   houses   want   near   summer

a Upper Swell is a pretty ^{1}_____ in the United Kingdom. It has a

lot of old ^{2}_____. There is also a river in the village with a

^{3}_____. You can sit and watch the water. It is very quiet but a lot of

people visit it in the ^{4}_____.

b The Adelaide Hills are in ^{5}_____. It is very lovely there. You can see

a lot of animals and birds in the wildlife ^{6}_____. The hills are

^{7}_____ the city of Adelaide.

c Barcelona is a big city in Spain, ^{8}_____ to the sea. It has a lot of

interesting buildings. Tourists ^{9}_____ to go there ^{10}_____

there is always a lot to do and see. This building is by Gaudi. Do you like it?

17  **Check (✓).**

1 Where is Champ?

2 Who put Champ there?

18 **Circle T = True or F = False.**

1 Serena opens the door with a key.   T / F

2 Serena has a pet cat.   T / F

3 There aren't any real pets in the future.   T / F

4 Zero Zendell has a zoo.   T / F

5 The children like Zero Zendell.   T / F

6 Chris and Marta don't want to rescue champ.   T / F

19 **Look at the picture of Serena's house. Read and draw.**

Hi! This is my house. It's small and it's noisy, but I like it. My favorite thing is the sofa. My TV is opposite the sofa. It's very big. There's a tall lamp between the sofa and the cupboard. My bed is opposite the cupboard. My robo-pet dog is on the bed. There's a small table in front of the sofa, between the bed and cupboard. On the table is my lunch— today it's pasta and chocolate cake. Yum!

20 Find and write.

3

Learn to be flexible. It's often frustrating to do what you don't want to do.

I want to ....

but I have to ....

1 I want to __meet my friends__ but I have to go to __the supermarket__ with my Dad.

2 I want to go to the _____ but _____ take my little brother to _____.

3 _____ play _____ go to _____.

4 _____ go to _____ _____.

5 _____ study for _____.

21 Match.

1	library	a	you can fly from here
2	behind	b	you can get books here
3	supermarket	c	you can play video games here
4	park	d	you can play catch here
5	hospital	e	not far away
6	airport	f	there are many trains here
7	arcade	g	this shop sells a lot of food
8	station	h	opposite of "in front of"
9	video store	i	you can get movies here
10	near	j	nurses and doctors work here

22 Listen and write the places. Then write the answers.

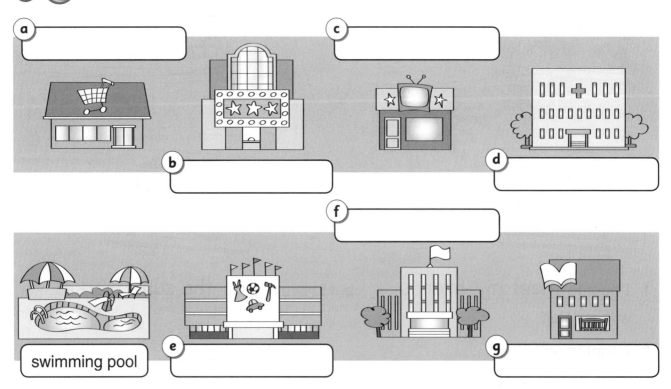

a

c

b

d

f

swimming pool

e

g

Where does she have to go?

1 the _____

2 _____

Where does she want to go?

1 _____

2 _____

23  **Listen and write.**

SEARCH

I live in a small town, but I like it. There aren't any shopping malls or movie

theaters, but there ¹_____ some restaurants and a lot of

²_____ stores. One good Chinese ³_____ is

⁴_____ my house. There is a supermarket, too. It is ⁵_____

the swimming pool. I ⁶_____ to go to the swimming pool tomorrow with

my friends. There is a ⁷_____, too. Sometimes I go there to get books.

The library is near my school—go straight from my house and ⁸_____

left. There is a small food store ⁹_____ my house, too. It is open late

so I can ¹⁰_____ get things when I want them.

24 **Write about where you live.**

Good days and bad days

1 Write. What is Flo's favorite food?

My favorite food is _____.

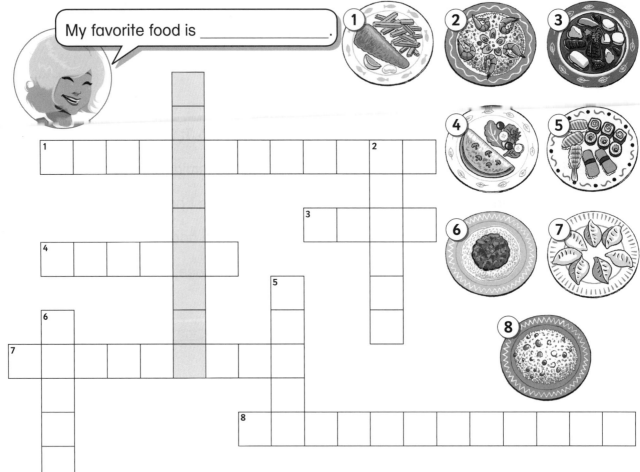

2 Write. Use words from Activity 1. Then circle.

Quiz

1 _____Spaghetti_____ is Italian.   Do you eat it?   Yes / No

2 _____ is Spanish.   Do you eat it?   Yes / No

3 _____ is Indian.   Do you eat it?   Yes / No

4 _____ is British.   Do you eat it?   Yes / No

5 _____ is Japanese.   Do you eat it?   Yes / No

6 _____ are Chinese.   Do you eat them?   Yes / No

3 ✎ **Write.**

1 climb _____climbed_____ 2 cook _____ 3 drop _____

4 want _____ 5 paddle _____ 6 fall _____

7 sail _____ 8 eat _____

4 ✎ **Write. Use words from Activity 3.**

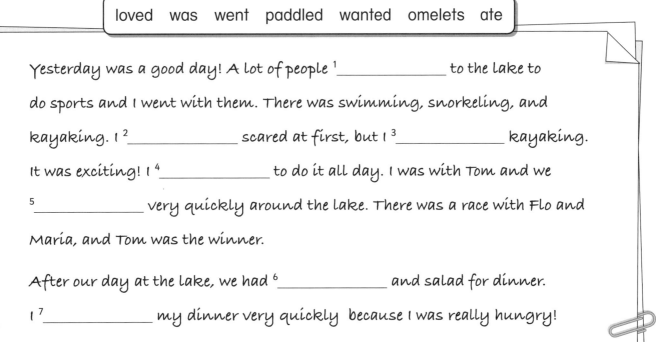

1

I _____ Mount Everest last year.

2

We _____ paella yesterday. It was difficult!

3

He _____ the plate on his foot. Ouch!

5 ✎ **Write. Then circle.**

| loved   was   went   paddled   wanted   omelets   ate |

Yesterday was a good day! A lot of people ¹_____ to the lake to

do sports and I went with them. There was swimming, snorkeling, and

kayaking. I ²_____ scared at first, but I ³_____ kayaking.

It was exciting! I ⁴_____ to do it all day. I was with Tom and we

⁵_____ very quickly around the lake. There was a race with Flo and

Maria, and Tom was the winner.

After our day at the lake, we had ⁶_____ and salad for dinner.

I ⁷_____ my dinner very quickly because I was really hungry!

Who is the writer?

Tom / Flo / Felipe

39

6 **Circle. Then match.**

a

c

e

1 miss (the bus / the bag)

2 eat (my juice / my lunch)

3 drop (the ball / the bus)

4 pass (a test / a curry)

5 pack (my test / my bag)

6 bring (my juice / my home)

b

d

f

7 **Circle.**

1 They were very hungry this morning so they (ate / didn't eat) some sandwiches.

2 Flo (missed / didn't miss) the bus yesterday. She was early.

3 Tom (dropped / didn't drop) the ball. He caught it.

4 Felipe (brought / didn't bring) his lunch. He had to buy lunch.

5 Last night, I (packed / didn't pack) my bag. I always pack it early.

6 I (passed / didn't pass) my science test last week. I'm good at science.

8 **Write.**

1

The woman _____ (like) the movie, but the boys _____ (love) it.

2

He _____ (play) soccer last week. He was sad because he really _____ (want) to play.

3

She _____ (put) a lot of food on her tray, but she _____ (drop) her lunch.

25 **Sing.** (See Student Book page 50.)

9 🎧 26 **Listen and number.**

a

b

c

d

10 ✏️ **Look at the pictures in Activity 9. Write the answers.**

a What happened? _____

b What happened? _____

c What happened? _____

d What happened? _____

11 ✏️ **Write about yourself.**

| brought / didn't bring   passed / didn't pass   missed / didn't miss   dropped / caught |

1 _____

2 _____

3 _____

4 _____

12 〔27〕 **Listen and match.**

1 Amy

2 Mark

3 David

a I went on holiday with my family.

b My family planned a party for me.

c I passed the test.

13 〔27〕 **Listen again and circle.**

1 Amy didn't want ….

   a a party   **b** a big party   **c** a surprise party

2 Amy's mom cooked ….

   a omelets   **b** curry   **c** spaghetti

3 Mark's test was ….

   a geography   **b** Spanish   **c** math

4 Mark's friends ….

   a passed the test   **b** didn't pass the test   **c** missed the test

5 David went ….

   a swimming and sailing   **b** swimming and surfing   **c** swimming and kayaking

14 **Write.**

1 He _____ to go to the park yesterday. He stayed home. (want)

2 They always _____ dinner at six o'clock. (cook)

3 I _____ the movie, but it was too long. (enjoy)

4 We always _____ our tests because we always do our homework. (pass)

5 She _____ the bus because she was late. (miss)

15  **Write.**

| dangerous | presents | filmed | funny | storms | laughed |

1 sailed, started, finished, phoned, enjoyed, _____, _____

2 scary, brave, boring, tired, sad, _____, _____

3 sailor, world, journey, waves, family, _____, _____

16 **Write.**

Yesterday was a really good day. There were no ¹_____

and the weather was good. I was ²_____ because

I ³_____ my family and friends. I ⁴_____

my Christmas presents, too. I ⁵_____ the funny presents and

the ⁶_____ .

17 **Imagine you're a sailor or explorer. Circle. Then write about a good day or a bad day.**

| sea | storm | happy | sad | scary | exciting | jungle | mountains |

Yesterday was a (good / bad) day. _____

_____

_____

 **18** Check (✓).

1 Who didn't go inside the zoo?

2 Who saw Champ?

 19 Correct the sentences.

1 Serena didn't visit the zoo last year.

_____

2 She liked the zoo.

_____

3 Serena didn't climb onto the roof.

_____

20 Write. Use the correct tense.

open   lock   drop   laugh   climb

1 He _____ his cage.

2 He _____ onto the table.

3 He _____ a chair on my head.

4 He _____ me in the cage.

5 He _____ at me.

(21) Write. What should they do?

Be positive about your day.
Don't worry. Be happy.

take a shower   rest   meet some friends
go to the movies   relax   do some exercise
go swimming   watch TV   call a friend   stay home
play some games   eat something you like   talk to someone

1

I took a test today. I have a bad headache.

You should take a shower and rest.

2

I studied math all day. I hate math!

3

I worked all day. My neck and shoulders hurt.

4

I worked all day. I need a break.

5

I got excellent grades today. I want to celebrate.

22 ✏️ **Match.**

1 curry
2 dumplings
3 stew
4 pack
5 spaghetti
6 drop
7 fish and chips
8 sushi
9 paella
10 omelet

a you use eggs to make this
b a hot and spicy food that is from India
c opposite of catch
d fish and rice—popular in Japan
e rice and seafood—popular in Spain
f a Chinese food
g a dish of meat and vegetables cooked slowly
h a type of pasta
i put things in a bag
j a popular food in the United Kingdom

I CAN DO IT!

23 💿 28 **Listen and number. Then write.**

a She _____ yesterday.

b They _____ a big _____ last year.

c We _____ stew for _____ today.

24 ✏️ **Unscramble and write. Then match.**

1 didn't / he / the / bus / miss

_____

2 didn't / sunglasses / bring / my / I

_____

3 catch / she / the / baseball / didn't

_____

a because it wasn't sunny.

b because he got up early.

c because it was very fast.

25 **29** **Listen and write.**

SEARCH

Last weekend was sunny. We ¹_____ soccer. We didn't win because our

goaltender ²_____ the ball many times and we ³_____ many

chances to score. After the game, I ⁴_____ home with my friends to have

dinner. My mom ⁵_____ stew, spaghetti, and chips. We ⁶_____

a lot of food! We ⁷_____ about the game and ⁸_____ our plan for

the next game.

26 **Write about what happened to you last weekend or last night.**

_____

_____

_____

_____

_____

_____

_____

_____

_____

_____

_____

_____

_____

5 Trips

1 **Write.**

_____ _____ _____ _____

_____ _____ _____

2 **Write. Use words from Activity 1.**

1 We went to the _____. There were a lot of fish there.

2 The _____ was great. We camped on Friday and Saturday night.

3 We loved the _____ because we love swimming.

4 I liked the _____. It was inside a big tent and there were funny people.

5 The _____ was great. I really liked the actors.

6 The _____ was fun. I was sometimes scared, but it was exciting!

7 The _____ was fun, but the queen wasn't there.

3 **Write about yourself. Use words from Activity 1.**

I love going to the _____ and _____.

I like _____

but I don't _____.

4 ✏️ **Write.**

1 I _____ table tennis last Wednesday.

2 They _____ to the amusement park on Saturday.

3 No, she _____ .

4 He didn't _____ to the park yesterday.

| went |
| played |
| go |
| didn't |

5 ✏️ **Look at Activity 4 and write the questions.**

1 _____ you do last week?

2 What did they _____ ?

3 _____ to the swimming pool?

4 _____ to the _____ ?

6 ✏️ **Unscramble and write.**

1 the / yesterday / did / go / you / to / supermarket

_____

2 went / ago / she / sports stadium / the / to / days / two

_____

3 on / the / didn't / bookstore / we / go / to / Saturday

_____

7 🔊30 **Listen and write ✓ or ✗. Then write questions and answers.**

① ② ③ ④

1 Did Maria go to the palace? _____   Yes, she did.

2 _____   _____

3 _____   _____

4 _____   _____

8 Write. Then find.

1

_____

2

_____

3

_____

a	r	o	l	l	e	r	c	o	a	s	t	e	r
p	m	i	n	i	a	t	u	r	e	g	o	l	f
i	z	b	s	e	r	c	f	p	q	j	d	i	g
r	b	f	e	r	r	i	s	w	h	e	e	l	k
a	u	s	a	r	e	m	v	a	w	y	z	t	k
t	m	n	y	g	o	s	d	t	c	l	u	s	c
e	p	k	a	q	a	h	i	e	e	d	h	n	l
s	e	i	h	g	b	c	a	r	o	u	s	e	l
h	r	l	p	f	n	x	d	s	o	b	e	v	t
i	c	m	z	n	f	w	m	l	f	b	n	k	j
p	a	w	q	t	b	k	u	i	r	g	u	p	x
x	r	o	v	y	j	c	u	d	l	v	m	w	t
p	s	z	p	a	d	d	l	e	b	o	a	t	s

4

_____

5

_____

6

_____

9 There are two more places in Activity 8. Find them and write.

My favorite ride is the _____.

I also like playing _____ with my friends.

10 Write. Then match.

| like   watch   play   go |

1 Did they _____ the chocolate cake?

2 Did they _____ soccer yesterday?

3 Did they _____ to the aquarium?

4 Did they _____ a funny movie?

a No, they didn't. They saw a scary one.

b Yes, they did. They loved the fish.

c No, they didn't. It was too rainy.

d Yes, they did. They loved it!

 **Match.**

1 What will you do at the library?
2 What will you do at the bank?
3 What will you do at the sports stadium?
4 What will you do at the museum?
5 What will you do at the aquarium?
6 What will you do at the national park?

a I'll get some money.
b First, I'll get some books for school. Then, I'll check the Internet.
c First, I'll go to the dinosaur room. Then, I'll go to the insect room.
d I'll see lots of beautiful fish.
e First, I'll pitch the tent. Then, I'll go kayaking.
f I'll watch a soccer game.

Write.

snorkeling   in-line skating   horseback riding
skateboarding   rock climbing   surfing

1

First, I'll go **snorkeling** _____

_____.

Then, I'll go _____

_____.

2

First, _____

_____.

Then, _____

_____.

3

_____

_____

_____

_____

13 **Write.**

amusement park   go   will   must   trampolining

Come to Adventure world!

You ¹_____ love Adventure world!

You will like our long, sandy beaches!

You ²_____ visit the famous ³_____!

In the evening, go in-line skating or ⁴_____!

You will never want to ⁵_____ home!

14 **Listen and circle.**

1 Oliver went to the (water park / amusement park).

2 The rides were (boring / exciting).

3 The weather was (rainy / sunny).

4 Oliver went (trampolining / in-line skating).

15 **Imagine you went on vacation last summer. Write.**

Hi, _____,

I'm in _____.

_____

_____

_____

Love,

_____

16 Circle and write your scores.

5

How beach-safe are you?

1 When it is sunny on the beach, you always wear a ....
- **a** bracelet
- **b** watch
- **c** hat

2 When you go to the beach, you always ....
- **a** bring sunblock
- **b** eat ice cream
- **c** wear your favorite jeans

3 When swimming in the sea, you ....
- **a** always swim near the beach
- **b** always swim far from the beach
- **c** never swim near the beach

4 Before swimming in the sea, you ....
- **a** always find the safe flags
- **b** wash your face
- **c** sometimes find the safe flags

5 When surfing in the sea, your surfboard is always ....
- **a** on the beach
- **b** next to you
- **c** far from you

1 a 0 points b 0 points c 5 points
2 a 5 points b 0 points c 0 points
3 a 5 points b 0 points c 0 points
4 a 5 points b 0 points c 0 points
5 a 0 points b 5 points c 0 points

20–25 points: You are very safe on the beach!
10–20 points: You are quite safe, but read the rules again!
0–10 points: Oh no! Don't go to the beach!

17 Write safety rules for the beach.

1 You should _____.

2 _____

3 _____

4 _____

18  Check (✓).

1 What can Marta, Chris, and Serena use to rescue Champ?

 **a**  **b** 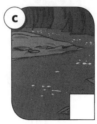 **c**

2 Who knows what is under the nature reserve?

 **a**  **b**  **c**

19  Write.

> closed   harbor   river   started   easy

1 Marta's parents _____ the nature reserve.

2 The nature reserve _____ 100 years ago.

3 There was an underground _____.

4 It was _____ to bring food for the animals.

5 The river went from the _____ to the nature reserve.

20 **33** Listen and number.

a water park _____ **b** palace _____

c aquarium _____ **d** amusement park _____

21 **Read Felipe's schedule. Then write.**

Plan, but be flexible. Planning helps you do more things.

Time	To do:
7:30	get up, shower, and have breakfast
8:30	meet friends in front of the camp
8:45	take a bus to the water park - go swimming - go on the water slide
12:00	lunch
2:00	go to amusement park - ride the roller coaster - play miniature golf
5:00	take bus back to camp

Tomorrow is the big day! We'll go to the water park and amusement park!

At 7:30, I'll get up, shower, and have breakfast. At 8:30, ¹_____

friends ²_____ the camp.

Then, at 8:45, ³_____

take a bus to the ⁴_____.

First, we'll ⁵_____. Then, we'll

⁶_____. At 12:00, we'll ⁷_____.

At 2:00, we'll ⁸_____. ⁹_____,

we'll ¹⁰_____. ¹¹_____, we'll

¹²_____. At 5:00, we'll take the bus back to camp.

22 **Plan how to review for an English test. Number in the best order.**

a Ask a friend to review. ☐

b Plan the work, and when and where to meet. ☐

c Read the "Look" boxes and check we understand them. ☐

d Find examples of the grammar in each unit. ☐

e Meet at the school library. ☐

VALUES

5

SEARCH

23  **Match.**

1 bumper cars
2 aquarium
3 paddle boats
4 amusement park
5 roller coaster
6 circus
7 pirate ship
8 national park
9 water slide
10 palace

a You can ride these on a lake.
b You can sail in this but not on the sea.
c This is a big natural area in the mountains or forest.
d Children can drive these.
e A king or queen lives here.
f This is fast and wet!
g You can see many types of fish here.
h This is a fast and exciting ride but not wet.
i This is usually in a big tent.
j This is a fun place. There are many rides here.

24  **Write.**

1 What did you do yesterday?

_____

2 What will you do tomorrow?

First, _____.

Then, _____.

25  **Unscramble and write questions. Then write the answers.**

1 supermarket / did / go / to / a / you / yesterday

_____

_____

2 mom / week / did / go / to / last / theater / your / a

_____

_____

3 did / a / circus / year / go / to / last / your / friend

_____

_____

26 🔊 34 **Listen and write.**

SEARCH 〰〰〰〰〰

Next week is our school trip. We [1]_____ on the bus at 7:30 a.m.

The bus trip [2]_____ about two hours. First, we will go to a

[3]_____. In the museum we will study [4]_____.

It will be interesting, I think. Then, we [5]_____ lunch in the

[6]_____ that is next to the museum. In the afternoon,

we will go to an [7]_____. It will be a lot of fun. First, I

[8]_____ on the [9]_____. Then, I'll go on

the bumper [10]_____ and pirate [11]_____ with my

friends. We will get home at about 8:00 p.m. My mom is coming to school to

[12]_____ the bus.

---

27 ✏️ **Write about somewhere you will go this year. What will you do?**

_____

_____

_____

_____

_____

_____

_____

_____

_____

6 Arts and entertainment

1 **Write.**

①

②

③

_____musical_____

④

⑤

⑥

_____   _____   _____

2 🎵35 **Listen and circle.**

1 Maria likes (romances / thrillers) because they are exciting.

2 She thinks she's too old for (cartoons / musicals) now.

3 Felipe loves (comedies / cartoons).

4 Maria loves (musicals / comedies).

3 **Write about which type of movies you like/don't like.**

I like _____ and _____, but I don't like _____.

I love _____ because _____.

4 Write.

Last week …

1 Tom ✗ make   <u>Tom didn't make a cake.</u>

2 Maria ✓ see

3 Felipe ✗ have

4 Flo ✓ write in   _Flo's diary_

5 Write.

| didn't   did   saw   was   had   went   jumped |

Yesterday was fun. I ¹_____ to the movie theater by myself.

I ²_____ a comedy. It was about a funny man, George. He

³_____ many things with his dog. George always made mistakes

but the dog corrected them. It ⁴_____ really funny. I ⁵_____

a good time. After the movie, I saw Maria. I ⁶_____ out but

she ⁷_____ see me!

6 Write.

1 She went hiking by _____ herself _____.

2 They went to school by _____.

3 You made breakfast for all the family by _____.

4 We wrote the song by _____.

5 He watched the movie by _____.

6 I played video games by _____.

7 Find and write thirteen music words.

q	z	c	o	u	n	t	r	y	c	o	b
c	e	a	p	b	r	l	u	f	v	g	h
l	t	a	m	b	o	u	r	i	n	e	a
a	y	a	d	c	c	e	l	l	o	c	r
r	f	o	z	e	k	n	t	j	d	k	m
i	t	r	i	a	n	g	l	e	t	h	o
n	p	o	p	n	o	k	a	j	f	b	n
c	d	c	d	t	p	i	h	i	v	b	i
t	r	r	l	h	a	r	p	i	g	l	c
b	u	m	l	m	a	w	q	l	u	u	a
s	m	s	a	x	o	p	h	o	n	e	n
x	s	r	j	a	z	z	w	j	e	s	k

1 _____
2 _____
3 _____
4 _____
5 _____
6 _____
7 _____
8 _____
9 _____
10 _____
11 _____
12 _____
13 _____

8 Write.

> tambourine   jazz   band
> saxophone   sing   sang   did

Bryn: Did you play the clarinet at the school music festival?

Michelle: Yes, I ^{1}_____.

Bryn: Did Jack and John play with you in the ^{2}_____?

Michelle: Yes, they did. Jack played the ^{3}_____ and John played the

harmonica. We played ^{4}_____ music.

Bryn: Did Alice ^{5}_____? She's your singer right?

Michelle: Yes, that's right. She ^{6}_____, and hit a ^{7}_____, too.

9 Look at Activity 8 and write the answers.

1 Did Michelle play at the school festival?   _____

2 What did she play?   _____

3 Did Alice play the saxophone?   _____

10 (37) **Listen and check (✓). Then complete Flo's diary.**

	make a cake	write birthday cards	say "Happy Birthday!"	go to the theater	see dancers
Flo					
Tom					
Mom					

My birthday last year was great. My mom ¹_____ a cake for me.

Tom ²_____ a nice birthday card and everyone ³_____

"Happy birthday!" I was very happy. Mom ⁴_____ tickets for the

theater and we all ⁵_____ the next day. We ⁶_____ dancers

and ⁷_____ some great music. I loved it!

11 (38) **Write. Then listen and complete for Cho.**

		Your answer	Cho
1	Have you ever written a letter in English?		Yes, she has.
2	Have you ever bought a foreign band's CD?		
3	Have you ever made dinner for your family?		
4	Have you ever been late for school?		
5	Have you ever lost your keys?		
6	Have you ever missed a train or bus?		

12  **Listen and circle.**

1 Alicia is talking about ….

a a song   **b** a book

2 The name of the book is ….

a *Inkheart*   **b** *Inkeyes*

3 The writer of the book is ….

a Fornelia Hunke   **b** Cornolia Funke

4 The name of the girl in the story is ….

a Alicia   **b** Meggie

Alicia

13 **Listen again and check (✓).**

	True	False	Don't know
1 It's about a girl, Meggie.			
2 Meggie and her dad love books.			
3 The monsters are scary.			
4 Meggie and Alicia are both 12.			
5 The book is short.			
6 Alicia didn't like the movie.			

14 **Write.**

> monsters   loved   saw   like   go   long   seen

1 I usually _____ to the movie theater on the weekend.

2 Yesterday, I _____ the movie *Inkheart*.

3 The movie is quite _____ but the story is really good.

4 I _____ most of the actors in the movie.

5 I didn't _____ the actress playing Meggie.

6 I have _____ that movie.

7 The _____ in the movie are interesting.

15 Find and circle ten words.

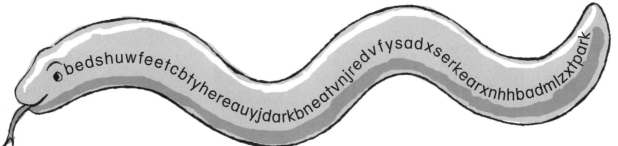

bedshuwfeetcbtyhereauyjdarkbneatvnjredvfysadxserkearxnhhbadmlzxtpark

16 Put the words from Activity 15 that sound the same together.

1   bed   red

2 _____ _____

3 _____ _____

4 _____ _____

5 _____ _____

17 Use the words from Activity 16.
Write two-line poems.

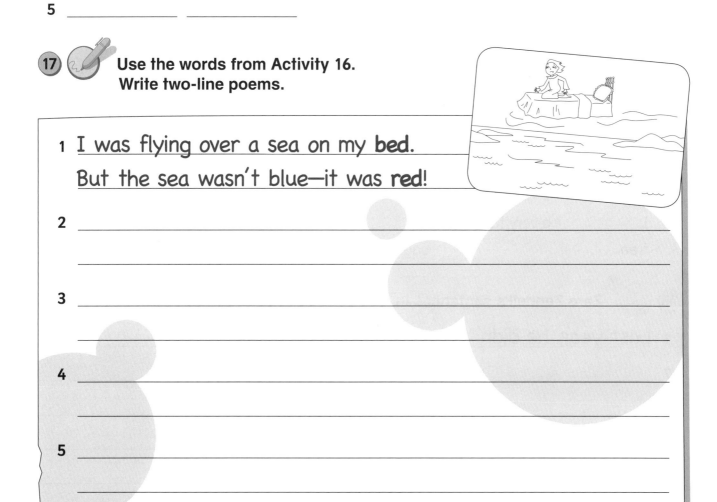

1 I was flying over a sea on my **bed**.
But the sea wasn't blue—it was **red**!

2 _____
_____

3 _____
_____

4 _____
_____

5 _____
_____

18 Check (✓).

1 Who is not telling the truth?

 a  b  c

2 Where did Zero Zendell find the chimp?

 a  b  c

19 40 Listen and write.

1

Last year, I _____ the Indian Ocean.

2

I _____ a mountain.

3

I _____ into the rain forest.

4

I _____ a very tall tree.

5

I _____ a special cage.

6

And I _____ the last dodo in the world!

20 Zero Zendell's sentences in Activity 19 are not true. Correct the sentences.

1 <u>Last year, he didn't cross the Indian Ocean.</u>

2 _____

3 _____

4 _____

5 _____

6 _____

21 Check *by yourself* (✓) or *as a team* (✓✓✓). Then write.

VALUES

Learn to be self-sufficient. You can always do some things by yourself.

1

| ✓✓✓ | They <u>are studying math</u> |

_____ as a team.

2

He _____

_____ by himself.

3

| | She _____ |

_____.

4

| | He _____ |

_____.

5

| | They _____ |

_____.

6

| | She _____ |

_____.

22 Write.

Things I like to do by myself	Things I like to do in a group
_____	_____
_____	_____
_____	_____
_____	_____
_____	_____

23 Match.

1	cello	a	You blow this instrument and it is very small.
2	harmonica	b	A type of music that sounds like a color.
3	saxophone	c	A band usually has some of these. You have to hit them!
4	triangle	d	You can shake this or hit it.
5	blues	e	This is a metal instrument that you blow.
6	clarinet	f	This music's name sounds like a place.
7	drums	g	This is a large string instrument.
8	tambourine	h	This is a metal instrument that has three sides.
9	country	i	This music is popular!
10	pop	j	You blow into this wood instrument.

24 Number to make a conversation.

a Yes, I did. ☐

b It was OK, but not great. ☐

c Did you go, Mike? ☐

d Did you two go to the GG99 concert last Saturday? ☐

e I wanted to go but there were no tickets. ☐

f How was it? ☐

25 Unscramble and write questions. Then write your answers.

1 concert / ever / played / you / a / in / music / have

_____

2 to / did / your / school / you / lunch / today / bring

_____

3 ever / concert / you / a / been / pop / have / to

_____

4 someone / you / ever / famous / met / have

_____

5 swim / sea / summer / the / did / last / in / you

_____

26 **41** **Listen and write.**

SEARCH

My ¹_____ book is "The Goblet of Fire." This is the ²_____ book

in the Harry Potter series. I ³_____ this book a few years ⁴_____

but I still like it. I like this book the best ⁵_____ there is a lot of action in

it and there are a lot of battles. In this book, Harry fights a dragon by

⁶_____—this part is really good. I ⁷_____ Harry Potter

⁸_____ I like the character Cedric Diggory, too. Cedric Diggory was

handsome and hard-working. He was a ⁹_____ character but he

¹⁰_____ in this book because Lord Voldemort kills him.

27 **Write a review of your favorite book.**

7 Space

1   **Match. Then write.**

1	tele	net	1	_____
2	astro	ar	2	_____
3	space	on	3	_____
4	mo	en	4	_____
5	pla	llite	5	_____
6	st	scope	6	_____
7	ali	naut	7	_____
8	co	ship	8	_____
9	sate	met	9	_____

2 **Match.**

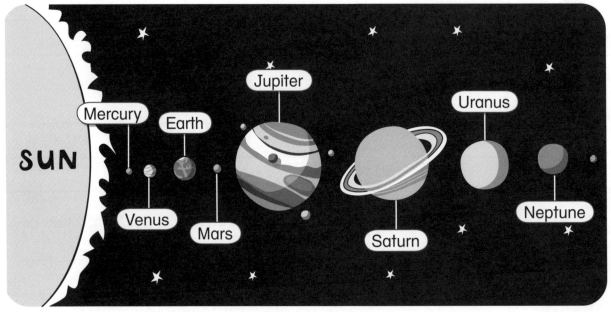

1 What is the third planet from the sun?
2 What is the second planet from the sun?
3 What is the eighth planet from the sun?
4 What is the fifth planet from the sun?
5 What is the fourth planet from the sun?

a Mars
b Earth
c Jupiter
d Neptune
e Venus

3 Write.

1 The astronaut is in the _____.

2 The astronaut is angry because there are _____ in the spaceship.

3 He doesn't know _____ they got in the spaceship.

4 Alien A has a _____.

5 Alien B is _____ on the astronaut's spacesuit!

4 Unscramble and write questions. Then match with the sentences in Activity 3.

1 a / telescope / who / has   <u>Who has a telescope?</u>   `4`

2 the / is / astronaut / where   _____   ☐

3 why / astronaut / the / is / angry   _____   ☐

4 doing / Alien B / what / is   _____   ☐

5 in / how / the / get / did / aliens   _____   ☐

5 Write five questions.

1 What's <u>the name of the biggest planet</u> _____?

2 Who _____?

3 Where _____?

4 When _____?

5 Why _____?

6 **Look at the table. Where do these words go? Write.**

> important   exciting   scary   frightening   tall   kind
> intelligent   difficult   pretty   complicated   small   clever

One or two syllables [big / ea-sy]	Three syllables or more [a-ma-zing]

7 **Read and write ✓ or ✗ for yourself.**

1 Sci-fi movies are more brilliant than cartoons. ☐

2 Soccer is more complicated than basketball. ☐

3 Amusement parks are more amazing than national parks. ☐

4 Elephants are more frightening than tigers. ☐

5 Math is more important than English. ☐

8 **Unscramble and write. Then circle Yes or No.**

1 more / brilliant / than / are / movies

_____ books.   Yes / No

2 Earth / amazing / the / more / than / is

_____ other planets.   Yes / No

3 more / snakes / frightening / than / are

_____ spiders.   Yes / No

9  **Write.**

1 Which are more intelligent, astronauts or doctors?

_____

2 Which is the most important, studying or exercise?

_____

3 Which are less exciting, amusement parks or video games?

_____

4 Which is the least complicated, science or math?

_____

10 **43** **Listen and write the price and weight. Then answer.**

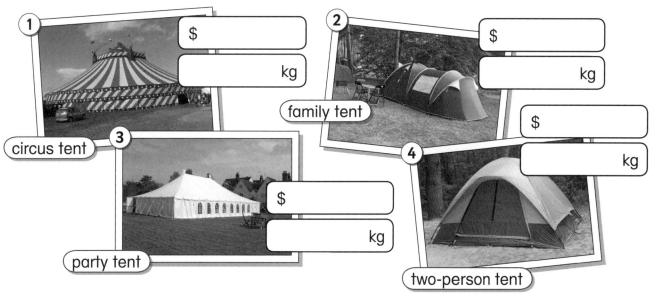

1 circus tent — $ ___ / ___ kg

2 family tent — $ ___ / ___ kg

3 party tent — $ ___ / ___ kg

4 two-person tent — $ ___ / ___ kg

1 Which tent is the least expensive?

_____

2 Which tent is more expensive than the party tent?

_____

3 Which tent is the heaviest?

_____

4 Which tent is the lightest?

_____

11 (44) **Listen, check (✓), and number.**

a The aliens thanked Jake. ☐

b Three days later, there was a postcard for Jake. ☐

c The aliens wanted to go to the fourth planet. ☐

d One alien said, "We're lost!" ☐

12 **Write the second part of Connor's story. Use the questions to help you.**

1 What did Jake see in the field? How did Jake feel?

Jake saw _____.

_____

_____

_____

2 What did the aliens ask Jake? What did Jake say? Where did the aliens want to go?

An alien asked, "Where _____"

_____

_____

_____

3 Did Jake dream about the aliens? What happened three days later? Was it a dream?

Jake went to bed and _____.

_____

_____

_____

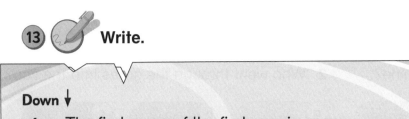

13 Write.

Down ↓

1 The first name of the first man in space.
2 Astronauts sleep in these.
5 Studying science is … for astronauts.

Across →

3 When you're in space you're body is ….
4 Use this to look at stars.
6 & 7 The names of the first two men on the moon:
… Armstrong and … Aldrin.
8 Jupiter is nearer to the sun
than this planet.

14 Can you remember the planets? Look at this phrase to help you.

Most Very Educated Monkeys Just Sleep Under Newspapers

Mercury Venus Earth Mars Jupiter Saturn Uranus Neptune

15 Write a phrase to help you remember the planets.

M _____   M _____   U _____

V _____   J _____   N _____

E _____   S _____

 **16** **Check (✓).**

1 Who went back in the time machine?

a

b

c

2 Who went through the gates into the zoo?

a

b

c

 **17** **Circle.**

1 Where does Serena go?

   a to the nature museum   **b** to the underground river   **c** home

2 What are the guards doing?

   a watching the show   **b** watching Serena   **c** sleeping

3 What does Serena find?

   a Champ   **b** a cage   **c** the time machine

4 Who is in a cage?

   a Zero Zendell   **b** Champ   **c** the guards

 18 **Unscramble the words and write.**

> ~~soiyn~~ twe tnigfrnghei dscear docl

a

They're _____noisy_____.

b

She's _____ and _____.

c

They're _____.

d

They're _____.

19 Match and then write. What materials can you use to make each model?

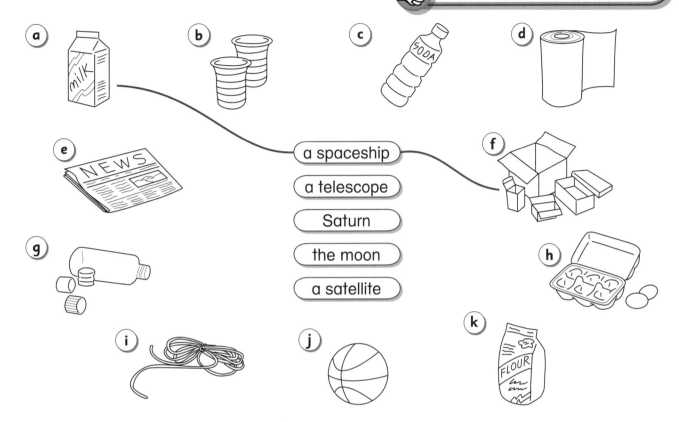

a milk
b
c SODA
d
e NEWS
f
g
h
i
j
k FLOUR

a spaceship
a telescope
Saturn
the moon
a satellite

1 We can build a model of a spaceship with: _____a and f_____

2 We can build a model of a telescope with: _____

3 We can build a model of planet Saturn with: _____

4 We can build a model of the surface of the moon with: _____

5 We can build a model of a satellite with: _____

20 Write. What do you think?

1 Which of the models in Activity 19 is the most complicated to build?

_____

2 Which of the models is the least complicated to build?

_____

3 Which of the models can you build?

_____

21 **Match.**

1 intelligent
2 amazing
3 complicated
4 frightening
5 important
6 a telescope
7 the moon
8 stars
9 satellite
10 comet

a scary
b the Earth has one
c bright things in the night sky
d something that you should do
e difficult to understand
f not natural but goes around the Earth
g this is bright and has a tail
h clever
i use this to look at space
j really, really good

22 **Write.**

1 _____ they?   They're aliens.

2 _____ they come from?   They came from Mars.

3 _____ they get here?   They came by spaceship.

4 _____ are you looking at the sky?   I think I saw a comet.

5 _____ that flashing light?   It's a satellite.

6 _____ you buy that telescope?   I bought it last week.

23 **Unscramble and write questions. Then write your answers.**

1   intelligent / whales / are / which / less / dogs / or

   <u>Which are less intelligent, whales or dogs?</u> _____

   My answer: _____

2   planet / which / most / the / interesting / is

   _____

   My answer: _____

3   science / more / is / or / English / which / difficult

   _____

   My answer: _____

24 **45** **Listen and write.**

SEARCH

Which sneakers are the best for me?

I want to buy some new sneakers. There are three pairs [1]_____ I like.

The [2]_____ pair is green with orange stripes. They look [3]_____

but they're the [4]_____ expensive at $105! The [5]_____ pair

is [6]_____ expensive. This pair costs $75. They look OK but the first pair

is [7]_____ beautiful. The [8]_____ pair is the [9]_____

expensive at $20, but they aren't a good fit. My mom says price is the most

[10]_____. But I think how they look is the most important!

25 **Choose three things to buy. Write about them. Compare price, size, and how they look.**

_____
_____
_____
_____
_____
_____
_____
_____
_____
_____
_____

8 The environment

1 Write.

| paper   recycle   turn off   reuse   use   garbage |

1

recycle _____

2

collect _____

3

_____ bottles

4

_____ plastic bags

5

_____ public transportation

6

_____ the lights

2 Write.

1 _____ people always reuse plastic bags.

2 _____ people sometimes reuse plastic bags.

3 _____ people usually reuse plastic bags.

4 _____ people never reuse plastic bags.

5 The total number of people was _____.

Do you reuse plastic bags?

(bar chart: always, usually, sometimes, never)

3 Write.

1 I _____ reuse plastic bags.

2 I _____ use public transportation.

4 (46) **Look at Tom's plans for next week. Listen and write.**

MONDAY	FRIDAY
1 Back to _____	**5** Call _____
TUESDAY	**SATURDAY**
2 Play _____ in the park	
WEDNESDAY	**SUNDAY**
3 Go to the _____	
THURSDAY	**NOTES**
4 _____ with Joe and Pete	

5 **Write questions about Tom. Then write the answers.**

> Is Tom going to go back to school on Monday?

> Yes, he is.

1 soccer / park / Tuesday _____

_____   _____

2 movie theater / Thursday _____

_____   _____

3 call / Joe / Friday _____

_____   _____

4 pizza / Thursday _____

_____   _____

6 **Write. What are you going to do next week?**

_____

79

7  **Match.**

1 What can you do to save trees?

2 What can you do to conserve energy?

3 What can you do to save resources?

4 What can you do to keep the planet clean?

a collect garbage

b recycle bottles

c recycle paper

d turn off the lights

8 **Write a green diary for next week. What can you do to save the Earth?**

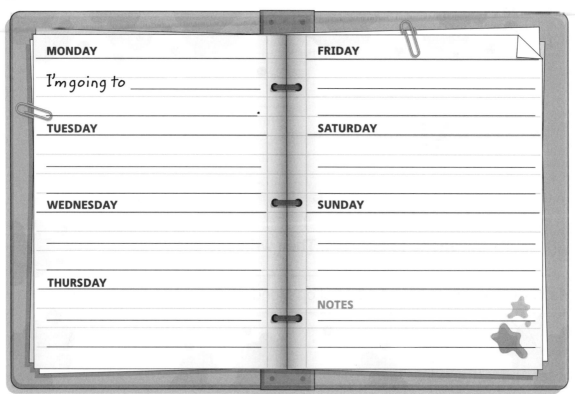

MONDAY

I'm going to _____

_____ .

TUESDAY

_____

_____

WEDNESDAY

_____

_____

THURSDAY

_____

_____

FRIDAY

_____

_____

SATURDAY

_____

_____

SUNDAY

_____

_____

NOTES

_____

9 **Write the words in the correct circle.**

waste   plastic bags   bottles   paper   pollution

Reuse

_____

_____

Reduce

_____

_____

Recycle

_____

_____

10 (48) **Listen and number.**

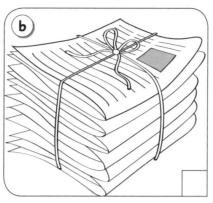

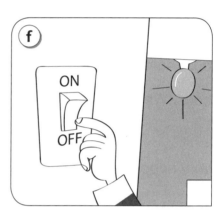

11 **Look at Activity 10 and write.**

a If you <u>recycle bottles</u>_____,

you'll <u>save resources</u>_____.

b If you _____,

you'll _____.

c If you _____,

you'll _____.

d If you _____,

you'll _____.

e If you _____,

you'll _____.

f If you _____,

you'll _____.

12 ✎ **Write.**

| buses | cleanest | garbage | plastic | tomorrow | bottles | going |

Hi Molly,

Your plans for ¹_____ sound fun! My class at school is going to have a Green Day. We're going to put all the ²_____ into different recycling bins and then we're going to make Green Day posters for school. I'm going to collect some garbage from home and others are going to bring paper, ³_____, and ⁴_____ bags. We're going to be the ⁵_____ school in our town! Then, we're all ⁶_____ to walk or cycle home—no cars or ⁷_____. I love cycling so I'm very happy! I'm going to like Green Day. Oh, and can I use your bike?

Thanks!

Niki

13 ✎ **Look at Activity 12 and write.**

1 What's special about tomorrow? _____

2 What's Niki going to make? _____

3 What does Niki want to borrow? _____

4 Is Niki a "green" person? _____

14 ✎ **Make lists.**

1 What are some of the causes of air pollution?	2 What are some kinds of garbage?
factories	soda cans
_____	_____

15 Find, circle, and correct each mistake.

Venezuela

1 The highest waterfall in the world is Angel Falls in (Chile). It's 979 metres high.

2 Australia is the smallest island and the smallest continent in the world.

3 The Atacama Desert in Chile, South America, is probably the wettest place in the world.

4 The Nile in Africa is the longest river in the world, and you can see it in five countries.

5 Mount Fuji is a very famous lake in Japan, and it's the highest mountain in Japan, too.

16 Circle.

Our amazing world QUIZ

1 Niagara Falls in the U.S. is ? than Angel Falls.

a higher	b 979 meters
c longer	d lower

2 Australia is the ? continent in the world.

a biggest	b 2nd biggest
c 3rd biggest	d smallest

3 The biggest desert in the world is the ? desert in North Africa.

a Gobi	b Atacama
c Sahara	d Arabian

4 The Amazon is the ? longest river in the world.

a 1st	b 2nd
c 3rd	d 4th

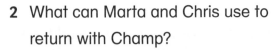

17  **Check (✓).**

1 Who got into the cage?

2 What can Marta and Chris use to return with Champ?

 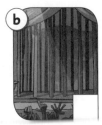 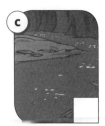

18 **Listen and match. Who said it?**

1 "Where were you?"

2 "We went to the amusement park."

3 "There are no real pets in the future."

4 "He was in a cage."

5 "We need to look after our animals."

19 **Circle or write you own answer.**

1 I think Marta is ….

  a brave

  b kind

  c _____

2 I think Zero Zendell is ….

  a mean

  b scary

  c _____

3 My favorite character is ….

  a Marta

  b Serena

  c _____

4 I think the story was ….

  a exciting

  b interesting

  c _____

20 Check (✓) the items you personally use daily. Then complete the diagram for yourself.

1 water ☐

2 electricity ☐

3 plastic cups ☐

4 batteries ☐

5 gas ☐

6 juice cartons ☐

7 milk cartons ☐

8 yogurt cartons ☐

9 writing paper ☐

10 soda cans ☐

11 wrapping paper ☐

12 plastic bottles ☐

13 food cans ☐

14 plastic bags ☐

15 paper bags ☐

16 cardboard boxes ☐

17 candy wrappers ☐

Save our planet. Learn to save energy and keep the planet clean.

I'll reduce ....

I'll recycle ....

I'll reuse ....

writing paper

21 Remind yourself what to do where. Complete the table below with items from Activity 20. Are there any differences?

	At school	At home
RECYCLE		
REDUCE		
REUSE		

22 **Match.**

1 conserve
2 reduce
3 recycle
4 turn off
5 pollution
6 public transportation
7 garbage
8 plastic bag
9 waste
10 energy

a a poison in the environment
b save or keep
c we use these to get food home from the shops
d buses and trains are two examples of this
e light and heat are two examples of this
f make less
g things that are used carelessly
h change into material that we can reuse
i things we throw away
j opposite of turn on

23 **Circle.**

I'm going to help make my school greener. My friends and I are ¹(will / going to)
put recycling boxes in every classroom. Then we can ²(collect / turn off) paper
and ³(transportation / bottles) to recycle. My family is also going to help
⁴(reduce / save) the planet at home. They're going to ⁵(use / turn off) the
lights when they go outside, and my mom is going to ⁶(use / reuse) public
transportation to go to the supermarket. We ⁷(will / going to) all be greener!

24 **Unscramble and write. Then match.**

1 public / transportation / if / you / use

_____

a you'll save resources.

2 collect / if / garbage / you

_____

b you'll conserve energy.

3 you / recycle / if / paper

_____

c you'll reduce pollution.

4 the / off / lights / if / you / turn

_____

d you'll save trees.

5 recycle / if / bottles / you

_____

e you'll keep the planet clean.

25 **50** **Listen and write.**

SEARCH ~~~~~~~~

Tomorrow, I'm going to be home late from school ¹_____ I have band

practice. This week we are ²_____ at lunchtime and after school. We

are ³_____ play in a concert ⁴_____ week downtown.

⁵_____ going to play the clarinet and my two best friends are going

to play the saxophone. ⁶_____ we play well, our teacher and parents

⁷_____ be very happy. My grandparents are coming and after the

concert we ⁸_____ going to go out for ⁹_____. It should be a

good evening. I ¹⁰_____ practice now!

26 **Write a journal entry about your plans for the future.**

At the weekend, I'm going to _____.

Then, I'll _____.

Next week, _____.

_____

_____

_____

Next year, _____.

_____

_____

_____

8

Goodbye

1 **Circle T = True or F = False.**

1 Marta is back from the future and lives with her parents. T / F

2 Champ is now living in the future with Zero Zendell. T / F

3 Chris is back in school studying hard. T / F

4 Serena is in Future Island walking her dog every day. T / F

5 Zero Zendell doesn't have a zoo now. T / F

6 There aren't any visitors to the zoo now. T / F

2  **Write.**

1 Whose is this?

_____

2 Why did he take it to the camp?

_____

3 Whose are these?

_____

4 What is in the photos?

_____

5 Who were in the bus?

_____

6 What did they see from the bus? _____

3 **Match.**

1 Were there any animals on Future Island?

2 What was Zero Zendell like?

3 Did the guards lock up Champ?

4 Who used the river to enter the zoo?

5 How did Serena break the cage?

6 Who got Champ from the stage?

a Yes, they did.

b Yes, there were but they were all in Zero Zendell's zoo.

c She used the time machine.

d He was a horrible man.

e Marta.

f Serena.

4 **Circle.**

1 What's Tom like? (Unit 1)

He's clever and good at (singing / sports).

2 Who cooked a stew? (Unit 4)

(Felipe / Flo) cooked a stew.

3 What will Felipe and Tom do first at the amusement park? (Unit 5)

They will go on the water (slide / park).

4 What was Flo doing near the park in Unit 3?

She was buying (chocolate / ice cream).

5 What were Flo and Tom doing on the hill in Unit 7?

They were having a (party / campfire).

6 Where are Tom and Flo from? (Unit 1)

They're from the United (States / Kingdom).

7 What does Hannah do to help clean up? (Unit 8)

Hannah (doesn't help clean up / collects the garbage).

8 Where's Felipe from? (Unit 1)

He's from (Spain / Mexico).

9 Where did Maria go in London? (Unit 5)

She went to the (palace / aquarium) and the theater.

10 What's Maria not good at? (Unit 1)

She's not good at (singing / surfing).

11 Who scared Maria outside the movie theater? (Unit 6)

(Felipe / Flo) scared Maria outside the movie theater.

12 What was Tom doing in Unit 2?

He was watching the (panthers / cheetahs).

13 What was Tom doing in Unit 8?

Tom was recycling (bottles / paper).

14 How many steps are there in the castle in Unit 3?

There are (450 / 540) steps in the castle.

5 Write.

My past

1 Last summer, I _____ .

2 Yesterday, I _____ by myself.

3 I've never _____ .

My present

4 I'm good at _____ .

5 I like _____ , but I don't like _____ .

6 I love _____ and _____ .

7 I can _____ , but I can't _____ .

8 There is a _____ my home.

9 I want to _____ .

10 I have to _____ .

My future

11 Tomorrow when I get up, first I _____ .

12 Then, I _____ .

13 Next year, I _____ .

14 If I study hard at school, I _____ .

6 Draw three animals. Then write about them.

1 The _____ is taller than the _____ .

2 The _____ is the _____ .

3 The _____ .

4 The _____ .

7 Write.

when   where   why   how   which   what   who

1 _____ are you happy?

2 _____ is that bright light?

3 _____ is the most frightening?

4 _____ is your favorite movie star?

5 _____ do you live?

6 _____ do you get up?

7 _____ did you get here?

8 Make a poster about how to help the environment. Then write.

1 I'm going to _____.

2 What can you do to help?

I can _____.

3 If you _____, you'll _____.

Welcome

Does it look good?	Yes, it does. / No, it doesn't.
What does it look like?	It looks good.
	It looks like a cake.

Unit 1 Adventure camp

Flo is good at swimming.
I like hiking, but I don't like sailing.
I love fishing and camping.

I'm pitching the tent.
We're putting in the pegs.
I can pitch a tent, but I can't read a compass.

Unit 2 Wildlife park

How heavy is it?	It's 800 kilograms.
How tall is it?	It's five meters tall.
The giraffe is taller than the rhino.	
The giraffe is the tallest.	

Are otters bigger than seals?	Yes, they are. No, they aren't.
Were the giraffes taller than the trees?	Yes, they were. No, they weren't.
Which is the heaviest?	The hippo is the heaviest.

Unit 3 Where we live

How do you get to the supermarket?
Turn left at the corner, then go straight.
The supermarket is behind the school.

I want to go to the park.	He/She wants to go to the park.
I have to go to the library.	He/She has to go to the library.

Unit 4 Good days and bad days

I cooked stew.	He dropped the plate.
She paddled very quickly.	We fell in the lake.

What happened?	I didn't pass my test because I didn't study.
	He didn't bring his juice because he was late for school.

Unit 5 Trips

What did you do yesterday?	I went to the aquarium.
Did you go to the aquarium?	Yes, I did. / No, I didn't.
Did you like the aquarium?	

What will you do at the amusement park?
First, I'll ride the Ferris wheel. Then, I'll go on the bumper cars.

Unit 6 Arts and entertainment

I saw the movie by myself.
You wrote it by yourself.
He made it by himself.
She didn't go to the movie by herself.
We didn't watch it by ourselves.
They didn't draw it by themselves.

Did you hear the cello?	Yes, I did. / No, I didn't.
Have you ever played the saxophone?	Yes, I have. / No, I haven't.
Have you ever been to a concert?	Yes, I have. / No, I've never been to a concert.

Unit 7 Space

Who are they?	They're astronauts.
When did they come?	They came last night.
Where did they come from?	They came from the moon.
How did they get here?	They came by spaceship.
Why are you looking at the sky?	I saw a flashing light.
What's that flashing light?	It's a spaceship.

Which telescope is more complicated?	The big telescope is more complicated than the small telescope.
Which telescope is the most complicated?	The big telescope is the most complicated.
Which telescope is less complicated?	The small telescope is less complicated than the big telescope.
Which telescope is the least complicated?	The small telescope is the least complicated.

Unit 8 The environment

Are you going to recycle paper?	Yes, I am. No, I'm not. I'm going to recycle bottles.

What can you do to help?	I can use public transportation.
If you reuse plastic bags, you'll reduce waste.	